Symbols of Canada

Capital Cities

Edited by Deborah Lambert

Weigl

Published by Weigl Educational Publishers Limited
6325 10 Street SE
Calgary, Alberta
T2H 2Z9

www.weigl.com

Library and Archives Canada Cataloguing in Publication data available upon request.
Fax 403-233-7769 for the attention of the Publishing Records department.

ISBN 978-1-55388-920-5 (hard cover)
ISBN 978-1-55388-926-7 (soft cover)

Printed in the United States of America
1 2 3 4 5 6 7 8 9 0 13 12 11 10 09

Editor: Heather C. Hudak
Design: Kathryn Livingstone

All of the Internet URLs given in the book were valid at the time of publication. However, due to the dynamic nature
of the Internet, some addresses may have changed, or sites may have ceased to exist since publication. While the author
and publisher regret any inconvenience this may cause readers, no responsibility for any such changes can be accepted
by either the author or the publisher.

Every reasonable effort has been made to trace ownership and to obtain permission to reprint copyright material. The publishers
would be pleased to have any errors or omissions brought to their attention so that they may be corrected in subsequent printings.

Weigl acknowledges Getty Images as its primary image supplier for this title.
Alamy: pages 13, 15, 17, 21, 22, 23 New Brunswick, 23 Northwest Territories, 23 Nunavut, 23 Saskatchewan, 23 Yukon.

We gratefully acknowledge the financial support of the Government of Canada through the Book Publishing Industry Development
Program (BPIDP) for our publishing activities.

Please note that populations and areas change frequently. Our information is based on the most current statistics available, which
are from the 2006 census, and refer to cities rather than metropolitan areas unless otherwise indicated.

Contents

Ontario

Northwest Territories

Saskatchewan

Prince Edward Island

Nunavut

Quebec

Yukon

What are Symbols?

A symbol is an item that stands for something else. Objects, artworks, or living things can all be symbols. Every Canadian province and territory has official symbols. These items represent the people, history, and culture of the provinces and territories. Symbols of the provinces and territories create feelings of pride and citizenship among the people who live there. Each of the ten provinces and three territories has its own capital city. It is a symbol of a province or territory's people and heritage.

Capital Cities of Canada

A capital is the city where the federal, provincial, or territorial government meets. The capital is not always the largest or most **populous** city in a province or territory. In many cases, the capital is the main centre of economic power for a province or territory. Capital cities in Canada were chosen for a variety of reasons, especially location and size. There are 14 capital cities in Canada. They include the national capital in Ottawa, 10 provincial capitals, and three territorial capitals.

Canada's federal government is located in Ottawa.

Locating Provinces and Territories

Each province and territory has a capital city. Each province and territory is unique because of its land, people, and wildlife. Throughout this book, the provinces and regions are colour coded. To find a capital city, first find the province or territory using the map on this page. Then, turn to the pages that have the same colour province or territory image in the top corner.

Web Crawler

Find out facts about
each province and territory at
http://canada.gc.ca/othergov-autregouv/prov-eng.html. Click on each province and territory.

Newfoundland
and Labrador

Quebec

Prince
Edward
Island

Ontario

Nova Scotia

New
Brunswick

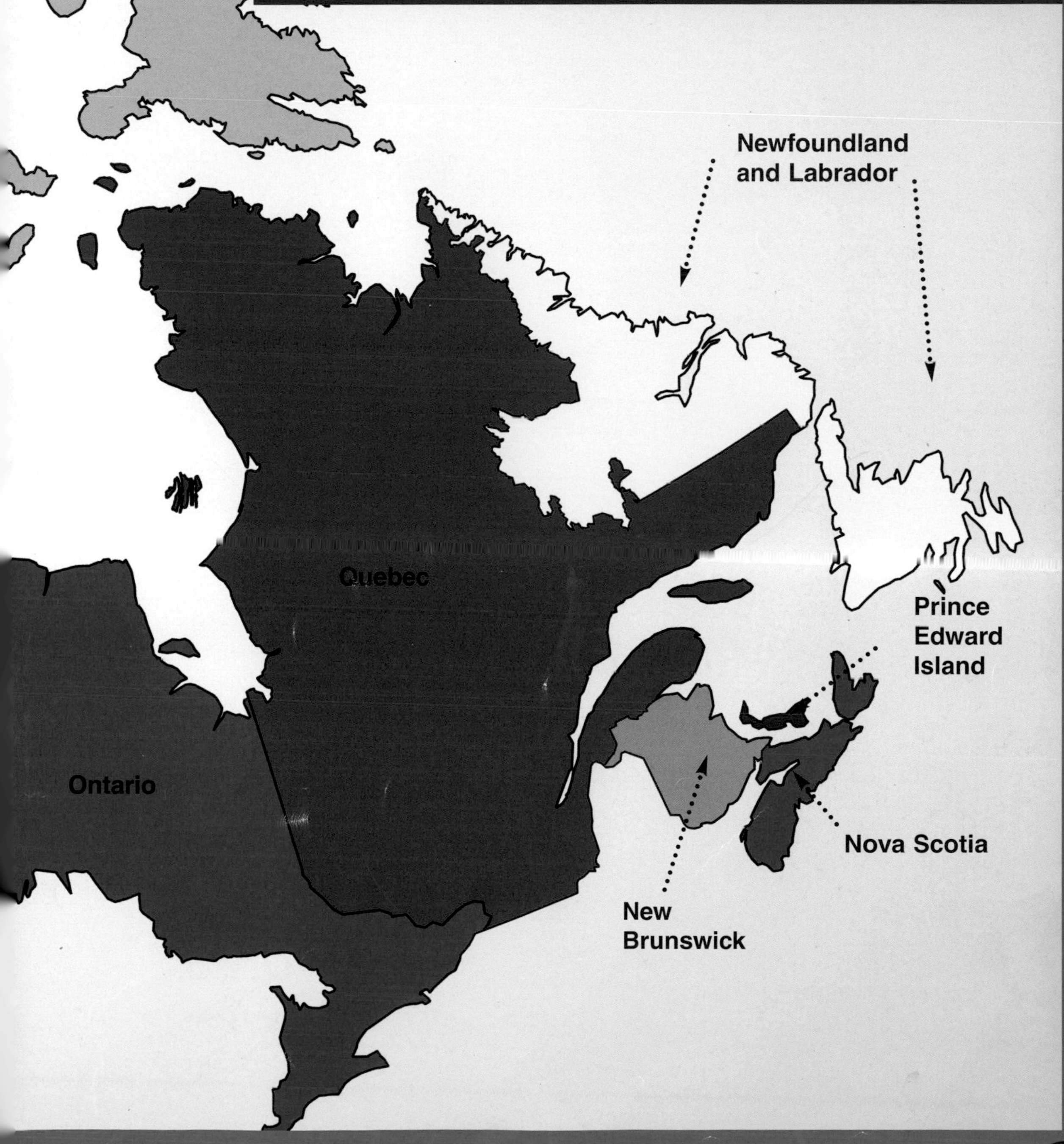

Canada's Land and People

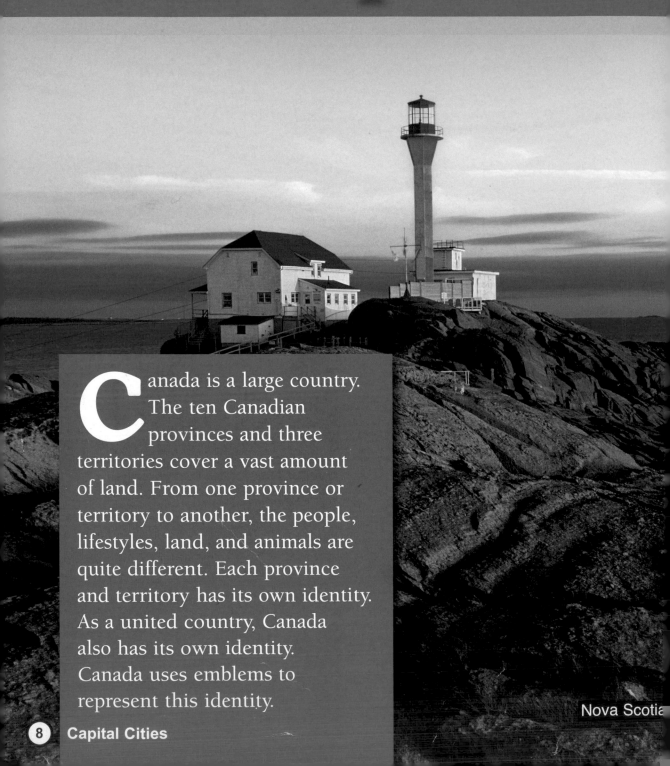

Canada is a large country. The ten Canadian provinces and three territories cover a vast amount of land. From one province or territory to another, the people, lifestyles, land, and animals are quite different. Each province and territory has its own identity. As a united country, Canada also has its own identity. Canada uses emblems to represent this identity.

Nova Scotia

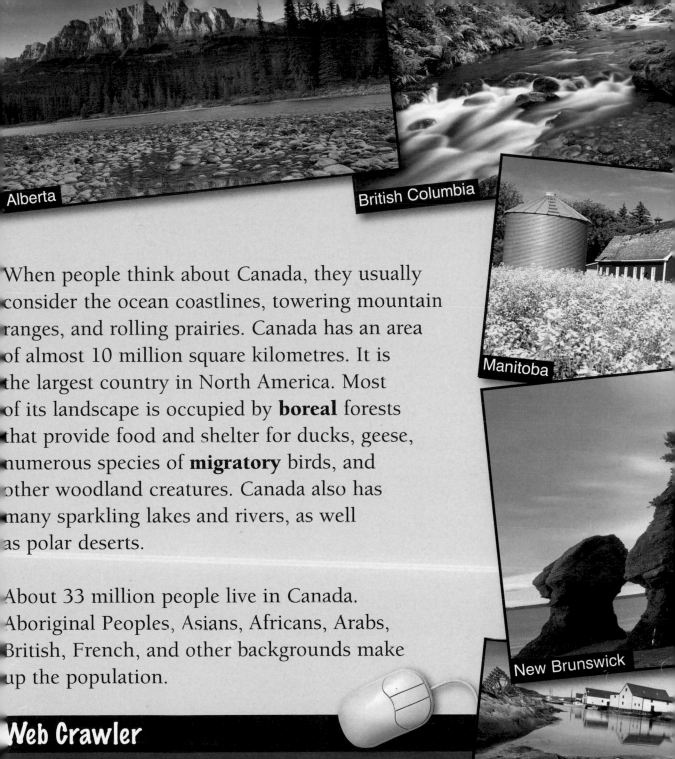

Alberta

British Columbia

Manitoba

New Brunswick

Newfoundland and Labrador

When people think about Canada, they usually consider the ocean coastlines, towering mountain ranges, and rolling prairies. Canada has an area of almost 10 million square kilometres. It is the largest country in North America. Most of its landscape is occupied by **boreal** forests that provide food and shelter for ducks, geese, numerous species of **migratory** birds, and other woodland creatures. Canada also has many sparkling lakes and rivers, as well as polar deserts.

About 33 million people live in Canada. Aboriginal Peoples, Asians, Africans, Arabs, British, French, and other backgrounds make up the population.

Web Crawler

Trace important events in the history of Canada at **www.cyber-north.com/canada/history.html**.

Discover Canada's natural wonders by clicking the numbers on the map of Canada at **www.thecanadian encyclopedia.com/customcode/Media.cfm?Params= A3natural-wonders.swf**.

Edmonton, Alberta

The Alberta Act of 1905 created Alberta out of a large piece of land called the North-West Territories. Edmonton was chosen as the temporary capital of the province, but several other communities, including Calgary, wanted to become the capital city. For the next few months, communities made presentations to the government in a bid to become the official capital. Edmonton was officially declared the capital of Alberta in 1906.

Edmonton sits in the centre of Alberta, next to the North Saskatchewan River. The city's name was taken from Fort Edmonton, a major fur-trading post that originally stood alongside Alberta's **Legislative** Building.

Edmonton has a land area of 684.37 square kilometres and a population of about 730,372. The city is known for its beautiful river valley, its festivals, its mix of cultures, and diverse economy. Edmonton has long been the transportation and distribution centre for Canada's northern communities, earning it the nickname "Gateway to the North."

Victoria, British Columbia

When British Columbia joined Canada in 1871, Victoria was the provincial capital. Located at the south end of Vancouver Island, the city was named after Queen Victoria.

Victoria has a population of about 78,057 and an area of 19.68 square kilometres. The city has a distinct British style and is known for its many gardens, as well as the whales, seals, and dolphins that swim in its ocean waters.

Aboriginal Peoples were the first to settle in what is now Victoria. Among them were the Songhee and Kosapsom. These peoples belonged to a group of Aboriginal nations known as the **Coast Salish**. In 1843, James Douglas, a British fur trader with the Hudson's Bay Company, arrived in the area. With his crew, Douglas built Fort Victoria, naming it for the British queen.

Victoria is a gateway to the **Pacific Rim**. Today, it holds many reminders of both its Aboriginal and British heritage. These are symbolized, for example, by a number of restaurants that feature British cooking and totem poles that stand where Aboriginal villages once stood.

Winnipeg, Manitoba

In 1870, Manitoba became the fifth province of the Dominion of Canada. That same year, Winnipeg was chosen as the provincial capital. Located in the southeastern part of the province, the city sits at the junction of the Red and Assiniboine Rivers. The name Winnipeg comes from the Cree words meaning "muddy water," referring to Lake Winnipeg, which is 65 kilometres north of the city.

Winnipeg occupies an area of 464.01 square kilometres and has a population of about 633,451. Together, Winnipeg and its outlying communities form **metropolitan** Winnipeg, which occupies 5,302.98 square kilometres of land. Winnipeg is one of the most culturally diverse capital cities in Canada. It is home to about 45 ethnic communities.

Winnipeg is the eighth-largest city in the country. Throughout the years, it has played a key role in the development of western Canada. It remains one of the country's main cultural, financial, and commercial centres.

Fredericton, New Brunswick

In 1785, Fredericton was chosen as the capital of New Brunswick. This city is located on the banks of the Saint John River in central New Brunswick and has an area of about 130.68 square kilometres. Being a **Loyalist** settlement, the city was named after Prince Frederick, the second son of King George III.

Fredericton was chosen as the capital of New Brunswick because of its excellent location. Although Saint John was a larger, more established community, its seaside location made it vulnerable to enemy attacks. In addition to being located farther from the Bay of Fundy, Fredericton can be easily reached by the Saint John River and is surrounded by forests and farmland.

Fredericton has about 50,535 people, who are mainly of Canadian or British origin. More than 20 percent of the population is **bilingual**, and about six percent is **Francophone**. For hundreds of years before Fredericton became the capital, the area was a seasonal stop for Maliseet and **Mi'kmaq** peoples. There, they hunted, fished, and grew corn and squash along the Woolastook, which was their name for the St. John River.

St. John's, Newfoundland and Labrador

In 1949, when Newfoundland and Labrador became the tenth province of Canada, St. John's was named the provincial capital. According to legend, the name St. John's is from the Feast of St. John the Baptist. It is believed that when explorer John Cabot first visited Newfoundland in 1497, he arrived at the time that this feast is celebrated.

Situated on the east coast of the Avalon Peninsula, St. John's surrounds a deep-water harbour that connects to the Atlantic Ocean via a long, thin channel known as "The Narrows." The city has an area of 446.04 square kilometres and a population of around 100,646. About one-third of Newfoundland and Labrador's entire population lives in the St. John's metropolitan area.

Today, St. John's serves as the commercial, cultural, and educational centre of the province. It is known for its colourful buildings, friendly people, and lively atmosphere.

Yellowknife, Northwest Territories

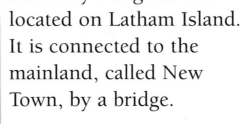

Yellowknife was chosen as the capital of the Northwest Territories in 1967. It is the only city in the Northwest Territories and is the second-most-northerly capital city in Canada. Yellowknife is located on the west shore of Yellowknife Bay, which lies on the north arm of Great Slave Lake.

Yellowknife covers an area of 105.22 square kilometres and has a population of about 18,700. It is the only community in the Northwest Territories that has a population of more than 5,000. Yellowknife is made up of two sections—Old Town and New Town. Old Town is the city's original townsite,

located on Latham Island. It is connected to the mainland, called New Town, by a bridge.

Yellowknife was named for the Yellowknife band of the Chipewyan nation. It had moved into the area to take part in the fur-trading industry. This band used knives that were made of yellow-coloured copper blades.

Halifax, Nova Scotia

Halifax was the capital of Nova Scotia in 1867 when the province joined **Confederation**. It is the largest city in Canada's Maritime Provinces and one of the oldest cities in Canada. Halifax is named after George Montagu Dunk, Earl of Halifax and Chief Lord of Trade and Plantations, who helped settle the area.

Halifax is located in central Nova Scotia, on the southern coast. It lies on one of the world's largest natural harbours and overlooks the Atlantic Ocean. Most of the city is located on a peninsula between the harbour and an inlet called the North West Arm. The City of Halifax became part of the Halifax Regional Municipality in 1996. It includes several counties and four **reserves**. The combined area is 5,490 square kilometres, with a population of 372,679.

Aboriginal Peoples lived in the Halifax region long before European explorers arrived. For hundreds of years, the Mi'kmaq hunted and fished the area's fruitful lands and waters. They called the region Chebucto, which means "the biggest harbour."

Iqaluit, Nunavut

Iqaluit, which means "many fish," is the capital of Nunavut, Canada's newest territory. In a **referendum** that took place in 1995, Iqaluit was chosen to be the capital of the new territory of Nunavut. However, it was only recognized as a city in 2001.

Iqaluit is the largest community and also the only city in Nunavut. With an area of 52.34 square kilometres, it is located on the southeastern part of Baffin Island, just north of Quebec.

Of all the capital cities in Canada, Iqaluit has the fewest people, with a population of about 6,184. Of this, about 60 percent are Aboriginal Inuit. The Inuit have been in the area for more than 500 years.

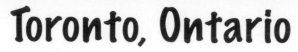

Toronto, Ontario

In 1793, Toronto was chosen as the new capital of Ontario. It was originally named York in honour of the Duke of York, George III's second son, Frederick Augustus. By 1834, the city had been renamed Toronto.

Toronto is located in the southern part of the province, on the north shore of Lake Ontario. The city covers an area of 630.18 square kilometres and has a population of about 2,503,281, making it the most populated city in Canada. Toronto is considered to be Canada's economic capital and is one of the top financial centers in the world.

The name Toronto was most likely derived from the Iroquois word *tkaronto*, which means "place where trees stand in the water." This refers to the northern end of what is now called Lake Simcoe. There, the Huron planted tree saplings to trap fish.

Charlottetown, Prince Edward Island

Charlottetown officially became Prince Edward Island's capital city in 1855. It is known as Canada's birthplace because the founding fathers first met there to discuss Confederation.

Charlottetown is named in honour of Queen Charlotte, the wife of King George III. The city is located on a broad harbour opening into the Northumberland Strait, which is on the south shore of Prince Edward Island. It has an area of 44.33 square kilometres and a population of about 32,174.

The first residents of Prince Edward Island were the Mi'kmaq. They named Prince Edward Island "Abegweit," which means "cradled on the waves." More than 2,000 years ago, the Mi'kmaq people hunted, fished, and farmed the area around modern-day Charlottetown.

In the 1800s, Charlottetown's major industries were shipbuilding and manufacturing. Among the city's biggest industries today are farming, fish and seafood processing, and tourism.

Quebec City, Quebec

Quebec City was named the capital of Canada from 1851 to 1855 and from 1859 to 1866. After Confederation, it became the capital of the province of Quebec. The name Quebec is from the Algonquin word *kebek*, which means "narrowing of the waters." This refers to the narrowing of the river at Cap-Diamant.

Quebec City has an area of 454.26 square kilometres. It is located 250 kilometres east of Montreal and 850 kilometres north of New York City. It has a population of about 491,142. Most of the people who live in Quebec City speak French, one of Canada's official languages.

In the early days of **New France**, Quebec City's most important trade was in furs and timber. However, in the 1800s, as a port city on the north bank of the St. Lawrence River, shipbuilding became a large industry. As one of Canada's most important deep sea ports, Quebec City still handles about 17 million tons of ocean-going cargo every year. The city is also an important destination for cruise ships, with more than 100 luxury liners docking there each year.

Regina, Saskatchewan

In 1905, Saskatchewan became a province, and Regina was named the official capital. The city has been called the "Queen City of the Plains" because *Regina* is the Latin word for queen.

Regina occupies an area of 118.87 square kilometres, and about 179,246 people call the city home. Located in the south-central part of the province, Regina is in the heart of Canada's prairie region. This makes it one of Canada's major prairie cities. In fact, the city seems to rise up like an **oasis** in the middle of the rolling prairies. Of all the cities in Canada, Regina is the one closest to the geographical centre of North America.

The Regina area was first inhabited by the Assiniboine and Cree. These early people named the area Oskana, which is a Cree word meaning "pile of bones."

Whitehorse, Yukon

Whitehorse became the Yukon's capital city in 1953. It serves as the financial, cultural, and commercial centre of the territory. Whitehorse is named after the White Horse Rapids on the Yukon River. The rapids were said to look like the manes of charging white horses.

Whitehorse is situated in the southern part of the territory on the west bank of the Yukon River, about 80 kilometres north of the British Columbia border. It covers an area of 416.43 square kilometres and is the most westerly capital city in Canada. About 20,461 people call Whitehorse home, representing about two-thirds of the Yukon's entire population.

People have been frequenting the Whitehorse area for thousands of years. More than 2,500 years ago, Aboriginal Peoples were setting up seasonal fishing and hunting camps in the region. These groups included the Southern Tutchone and Tagish peoples of the Yukon interior, and the Tlingit peoples from the Pacific coast.

Guide to Canada's Capitals

THE NATIONAL CAPITAL
Ottawa

ALBERTA
Edmonton

BRITISH COLUMBIA
Victoria

MANITOBA
Winnipeg

NEW BRUNSWICK
Fredericton

NEWFOUNDLAND AND LABRADOR
St. John's

NORTHWEST TERRITORIES
Yellowknife

NOVA SCOTIA
Halifax

NUNAVUT
Iqaluit

ONTARIO
Toronto

PRINCE EDWARD ISLAND
Charlottetown

QUEBEC
Quebec City

SASKATCHEWAN
Regina

YUKON
Whitehorse

Canada's National Capital

National emblems are symbols that are used for the entire country. The Canadian flag, known as the Maple Leaf, is one such symbol. Another is the common loon, which is the national bird. The maple is the national tree. The capital of Canada is Ottawa.

Ottawa was originally called Bytown after Colonel John By of the Royal Engineers. He supervised the building of the Rideau Canal.

The name "Ottawa" comes from the Algonquin word *Odawa*, meaning "traders."

Ottawa is known for its tulips, museums, high-technology companies, and its green-roofed Parliament Buildings.

History of the Capital

In 1855, Bytown became an official city and was given the name Ottawa. Two years later, in 1857, Great Britain's Queen Victoria chose Ottawa as the capital of Upper and Lower Canada, now Ontario and Quebec. The queen's choice puzzled many people. They thought a city farther south would be better. Toronto and Montreal, for instance, had more people, kinder climates, and better transportation links. Despite these concerns, the Parliament Buildings were built in Ottawa. In 1867, when Canada was born, Ottawa became the nation's capital.

Parts of Parliament Hill

O ttawa's Parliament Hill is one of the most significant heritage sites in Canada and a symbol of national pride for Canadians.

THE CENTRE BLOCK
The Centre Block houses the Senate, the House of Commons, and the Library of Parliament. Many important offices, such as the prime minister's office, are also in the Centre Block.

WEST BLOCK The West Block houses ministers' offices, members of parliament, their employees, committee rooms, and the Confederation Room.

THE EAST BLOCK The East Block houses many senators' offices. The office of the first prime minister of Canada, Sir John A. Macdonald, also can be found here.

PEACE TOWER The Peace Tower is situated in the front of the Centre Block. It was named the Peace Tower to honour the Canadian men and women who sacrificed their lives in armed conflicts.

LIBRARY The Library of Parliament provides information, reference, and research services to senior Senate and House of Commons officials, parliamentarians and their staff, parliamentary committees, and associations and delegations.

Test Your Knowledge

1 What is a capital city?

2 Where is the city of Victoria located?

3 What is the meaning of "Winnipeg" in Cree?

4 Which capital city is called Canada's Gateway to the North?

5 Where is Fredericton located?

6 Which capital city is the eighth largest city in Canada?

7 Which two cities were named capital cities in 1906?

8 Which province was the tenth to join Confederation?

Which capital city is the largest city in Canada's Maritime Provinces?

13

Who were the first people to settle in Quebec City?

14

Which European first visited Newfoundland?

10

How did Yellowknife get its name?

15

Which capital city is known as Canada's Birthplace?

11

In which year was Iqaluit recognized as a city?

12

Which capital city is Canada's most populated city?

Create Your Own Symbolic Building

Create a symbolic building to represent your community. Begin by thinking about your community's history. What type of building would you want? Use this book to help you. What does the capital building in your province or territory look like? How will your design be the same as this symbolic building in your community? How will it be different?

Think about how your building will look. Will it have a dome? Will it be large or small? Where will you construct your building? Why? Look at the pictures in this book for help. You can also take a tour of Parliament Hill online at **http://revver.com/video/ 914042/parliament-hill-in-ottawa** or **www.parliamenthill.gc. ca/index-eng.html**.

Draw your building on a piece of paper. Use the diagram on pages 26 and 27 to help you design the parts of your building. Colour your drawing with felt markers. When you are finished, label the parts of your building.

Write a description of your building. What kind of building is it? What does it say about your community?

Further Research

Many books and websites provide information on capital buildings. To learn more about these buildings, borrow books from the library, or surf the Internet.

Books

Most libraries have computers that connect to a database for researching information. If you input a key word, you will be provided with a list of books in the library that contain information on that topic. Nonfiction books are arranged numerically, using their call number. Fiction books are organized alphabetically by the author's last name.

Websites

Find fun facts about each of Canada's provinces and territories at **www.pco-bcp.gc.ca/aia/index.asp?lang=eng&page=provterr&sub=map-carte&doc=map-carte-eng.htm**.

Learn about other symbols in Canada at **www.patrimoinecanadien.gc.ca/pgm/ceem-cced/symbl/index-eng.cfm**.

To learn about other buildings in Toronto, visit **www.emporis.com/en/wm/ci/bu/mf/?id=100993**.

Glossary

bilingual: able to speak two languages

boreal: northern regions with very cold temperatures

Coast Salish: an Aboriginal nation living on Vancouver Island

Confederation: the joining of the provinces and territories to form Canada

Francophone: a French-speaking person, especially in a region where two or more languages are spoken

legislative: having the power to make laws

Loyalist: one who is loyal or patriotic to the sovereign or government

metropolitan: consisting of a large city and its suburbs

migratory: to move from one place to another

Mi'kmaq: some of the earliest known inhabitants of eastern Canada

New France: the name for the French territories in North America until 1763

oasis: a fertile patch in a desert

Pacific Rim: the countries and land masses surrounding the Pacific Ocean

populous: having a large population

referendum: a general vote made by the people of a country for or against a particular government proposal

reserves: land set aside for Aboriginal Peoples

Index